reading proxy statements

A Guide to the New SEC Disclosure Rules for Executive and Director Compensation

Thomas M. Haines

About WorldatWork*

WorldatWork (www.worldatwork.org) is an international association of human resources professionals focused on attracting, motivating and retaining employees. Founded in 1955, WorldatWork provides practitioners with knowledge leadership to effectively implement total rewards – compensation, benefits, work-life, performance and recognition, development and career opportunities – by connecting employee engagement to business performance. WorldatWork supports its 30,000 members and customers in 30 countries with thought leadership, education, publications, research and certification. The WorldatWork group of registered marks includes: WorldatWork®, workspan®, Certified Compensation Professional or CCP®, Certified Benefits Professional® or CBP, Global Remuneration Professional or GRP®, Work-Life Certified Professional or WLCP™, WorldatWork Society of Certified Professionals®, and Alliance for Work-Life Progress® or AWLP®.

WorldatWork.
The Total Rewards Association™

WorldatWork
14040 N. Northsight Blvd., Scottsdale, AZ 85260
480/951-9191   Fax 480/483-8352
www.worldatwork.org

WorldatWork Staff Contributors:

Publishing Manager: Dan Cafaro
Executive Editor: Don Lindner, CCP, CBP, GRP
Contributing Editor: Christina Fuoco
Editorial Assistant: Wendy Anderson
Cover Design: Jamie Hernandez
Production: Deb Shenenberg

Table of Contents

Introduction

During 2006, the Securities and Exchange Commission (SEC) proposed and adopted extensive amendments to the proxy disclosure rules for executive and director compensation. The amended disclosure rules are intended to provide investors with a clearer and more complete picture of executive and director compensation than existed under prior disclosure rules, which were criticized as being too rigid in terms of format and inadequate in terms of all inclusiveness. The amended disclosure rules accomplish this by combining a revised and broader-based tabular presentation with an improved narrative disclosure that supplements the tables.

The new disclosure rules begin with a narrative providing a general overview of the executive compensation program, referred to as Compensation Discussion and Analysis. As the name implies, this disclosure requires a discussion and analysis of the material factors underlying the executive compensation policies and decisions that are reflected in the amounts reported in the tables that follow. In a separate corporate governance section of the proxy statement, the rules require a scaled-down version of the compensation committee report as well as other compensation committee governance disclosures, such as the committee charter, the processes and procedures for the consideration and determination of executive and director compensation, committee interlocks with company executives, and the use of executive officers and compensation consultants in the compensation determination process. The stock performance graph that existed under prior disclosure rules is retained under the rules, but it is moved to a separate section of the company's Form 10-K and is no longer considered part of executive compensation disclosure.

Following the Compensation Discussion and Analysis, the rules require a detailed disclosure of executive compensation that is organized in three broad categories. The first category is a presentation of total compensation for the last and next preceding two completed fiscal years, as reflected in a revised Summary Compensation Table. The Summary Compensation Table is supplemented for the last completed fiscal year by a new Grants of Plan-Based Awards table that provides back-up information for equity and incentive plan awards. The second category is a presentation of holdings of equity-related interests, as reflected in an Outstanding Equity Awards at Fiscal Year-End table that is intended to shed light on potential sources of future gains from previous equity awards. Also required is an Options Exercised and Shares Vested table that summarizes realization of these equity award gains during the last completed fiscal year. The third category is a presentation of retirement and other post-employment compensation, as reflected in a revised Pension Benefits table and new Nonqualified Deferred Compensation table and a narrative summarizing potential payments upon employment termination or change in control. Finally, the rules require a Director Compensation table and accompanying narrative disclosure that is similar to the Summary Compensation Table for executives.

The rules are applicable to registration statements, proxy statements and annual reports filed for fiscal years ending on or after Dec. 15, 2006. The discussion that follows is directed toward publicly held domestic companies that are not considered to be small business issuers, as defined by the SEC. Small business issuers, which at the time of this publication are defined generally as domestic or Canadian companies with revenues and market capitalization of less than $25 million, are subject to separate executive and director compensation rules that are intended to be less complex and burdensome than the rules that follow.

Compensation
Disclosure Framework

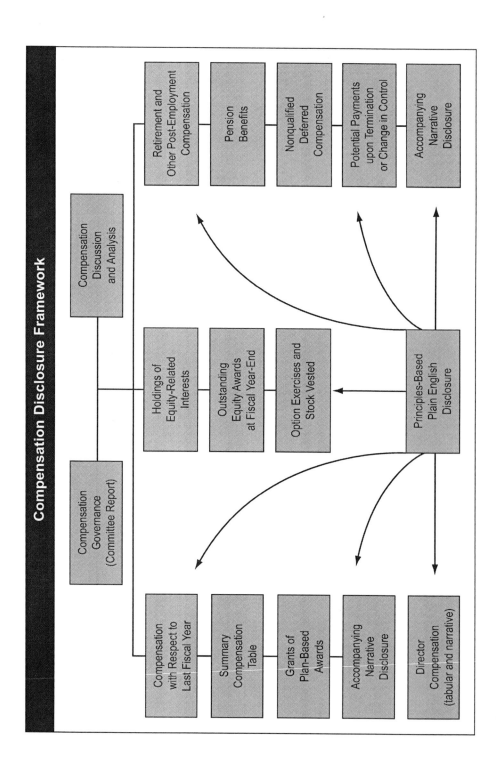

Compensation Disclosure Framework

Compensation Discussion and Analysis

Compensation Governance (Committee Report)

Holdings of Equity-Related Interests
- Outstanding Equity Awards at Fiscal Year-End
- Option Exercises and Stock Vested

Retirement and Other Post-Employment Compensation
- Pension Benefits
- Nonqualified Deferred Compensation
- Potential Payments upon Termination or Change in Control
- Accompanying Narrative Disclosure

Compensation with Respect to Last Fiscal Year
- Summary Compensation Table
- Grants of Plan-Based Awards
- Accompanying Narrative Disclosure
- Director Compensation (tabular and narrative)

Principles-Based Plain English Disclosure

Principles-Based
Plain English Disclosure

The disclosure rules are principles based, meaning that they set forth broad disclosure concepts and provide various examples to illustrate those concepts. In addition, the rules require companies to apply plain English principles when preparing executive and director compensation disclosures, as summarized below and on the following page.

What Companies Should Do

- Present information in clear, concise sections, paragraphs and sentences

- Use short sentences

- Use definite, concrete, everyday words

- Use the active voice

- Avoid multiple negatives

- Use descriptive headings and subheadings

- Use a tabular presentation or bullet lists for complex material wherever possible

- Avoid legal jargon and highly technical business and other terminology

- Avoid frequent reliance on glossaries or defined terms as the primary means of explaining information

- Use tables, schedules, charts and graphic illustrations that present relevant data in an understandable manner; graphs and charts must be drawn to scale and consistent with applicable disclosure requirements

What Companies Should Avoid

- Using legalistic or overly complex presentations that make the substance of the disclosure difficult to understand
- Using vague "boilerplate" explanations that are imprecise and readily subject to different interpretations
- Using complex information copied directly from legal documents without any clear and concise explanation of the provisions
- Repeating the same information in several places in the document unless doing so enhances the quality of the information
- Using tables or other design elements that are misleading

Companies are encouraged to use additional tables wherever tabular presentation facilitates clearer and more concise disclosure, such as a supplemental table for the all other compensation column (i) of the Summary Compensation Table, or a breakdown of director's fees for the Director Compensation table.

Named
Executive Officers

A n important principle underlying the disclosures applicable to executive compensation is that the disclosures are required only for named executive officers. The rules identify the following individuals as named executive officers:

- All individuals serving as the principal executive officer (PEO) and principal financial officer (PFO) during the last completed fiscal year (or acting in a similar capacity), regardless of total compensation level and whether they were serving as PEO or PFO on the last day of the last completed fiscal year.

- The three most highly compensated executive officers other than the PEO and PFO serving at the end of the last completed fiscal year, provided total compensation exceeds $100,000.

- Up to two additional former executive officers who would have been included in the top three categories above, except that they were not serving as executive officers at the end of the last completed fiscal year.

Compensation rank is determined by reference to total compensation for the last completed fiscal year, and is calculated by subtracting the pension and above-market interest amounts reported in column (h) from the total amount reported in column (j) of the Summary Compensation Table. It may be appropriate to include as a named executive officer one or more executive officers of a subsidiary or other employees who perform significant policy-making functions. It may also be appropriate in limited circumstances to exclude as a named executive officer individuals (other than the PEO or PFO) who rank among the most highly compensated due to payments relating to overseas assignments. However, other payments that are not recurring and unlikely to continue must be included in the named executive officer determination. Compensation information should be reported for the full fiscal year for any PEO, PFO or any other named executive officer that served as an executive officer for any part of a fiscal year.

Compensation Committee Governance

The rules consolidate disclosure requirements regarding director independence and related corporate governance disclosures in a separate section of the proxy statement. The disclosure rules specifically applicable to the compensation committee focus on the company's corporate governance structure that is in place for considering and determining executive and director compensation, such as the scope of authority of the compensation committee and others in making these determinations, as well as the resources utilized by the committee. These compensation committee governance disclosure requirements are summarized below:

- State whether or not the compensation committee has a charter. If so, make a current copy available through the company's Web site or as an appendix to the proxy statement at least once every three years. If the company does not have a compensation committee, state the basis for not having one and identify each director who participates in executive and director compensation decisions.

- Provide a narrative description of the company's processes and procedures for the consideration and determination of executive and outside director compensation, including the following:

  - Scope of authority of the compensation committee

  - Extent to which the compensation committee may delegate authority, specifying what authority and to whom

- Role of executive officers in determining or recommending amount or form of executive and director compensation
- Role of compensation consultants in determining or recommending amount or form of executive and director compensation
- If compensation consultants are involved in determining or recommending the amount or form of executive and director compensation, provide the following additional information:
  - Identify such consultants
  - State if they are engaged directly by compensation committee, or by another person
  - Describe nature and scope of assignment
  - Describe material elements of instructions or directions given to consultants with respect to performance of engagement duties.
- Under the caption "Compensation Committee Interlocks and Insider Participation" identify each person who served as a member of the compensation committee during the last completed fiscal year, indicating each member who:
  - Is an officer or employee of the company
  - Has any relationship requiring related party disclosure pursuant to Item 404 of Regulation S-K
  - Has an interlocking compensation committee/board relationship with an executive officer of the company.
- Under the caption "Compensation Committee Report" state if the compensation committee has reviewed and discussed the Compensation Discussion and Analysis with management, and based on that review and discussion,

has recommended to the board of directors its inclusion in the proxy statement or annual report.

♦ The names of each member of the compensation committee must appear below the Compensation Committee Report.

♦ The Compensation Committee Report is not deemed to be soliciting material or to be filed with the SEC.

♦ The principal executive officer and principal financial officer will be able to look to the Compensation Committee Report in providing their required certifications under the Sarbanes-Oxley Act of 2002.

In contrast to the compensation committee governance disclosures, the Compensation Discussion and Analysis discussed next focuses on material information about the compensation policies and objectives of the company's executive compensation program and seeks to put the quantitative tabular disclosure about named executive officer compensation into perspective.

Compensation
Discussion and Analysis

The purpose of Compensation Discussion and Analysis is to provide material information that is necessary to gain an understanding of the compensation policies and decisions regarding the named executive officers. The discussion should focus on the material principles underlying executive compensation policies and decisions and the most important factors relevant to analysis of those policies and decisions, without resorting to boilerplate language and repetition of more detailed information set forth in the tables, footnotes and narrative disclosures that follow. The discussion and analysis must address the following with respect to the executive compensation program:

- Objectives of the program
- What the program is designed to reward
- Each element of compensation
- Why each element is chosen
- How the amount of each element is determined
- How each element is linked to program objectives and other pay elements

It is expected that the material factors discussed and analyzed will vary depending on the facts and circumstances, but the rules are principles-based and set forth various examples of information that may be disclosed, including:

- Allocation between long-term and short-term compensation
- Allocation between cash and noncash compensation and different forms of noncash compensation

- Allocation between different types of long-term compensation, including cost/benefit analysis
- Determination of cash and equity award grant dates
- Use of performance measures
- Exercise of discretion, either to provide relief in event of failure to attain performance goals, or to increase/decrease payments
- Use of individual performance
- Adjustment or recovery of previous payments in event of financial restatement
- Increases or decreases in compensation materially
- Consideration of realized/unrealized prior compensation amounts in determination of retirement benefits
- Selection of award payment triggers in event of employment termination or change in control
- Consideration of accounting and tax rules
- Stock ownership requirements/guidelines and risk hedging policies
- Consideration of compensation benchmarking practices
- Role of executive officers in determining compensation

If the company has a program, plan or practice to time stock option grants to executives in coordination with the release of material nonpublic information, the discussion and analysis should address the following questions:

- Are grants to executives timed in coordination with the release of material nonpublic information?
- Are grants to nonexecutives similarly timed? If not, why not?
- What is the role of the compensation committee in approving and administering the timed grants?

- How did the compensation committee take such information into account when determining if and in what amounts to make grants?

- Did the compensation committee delegate any aspect of the actual administration of the program to any other persons?

- What is the role of executive officers in the company's practice of option timing?

- Does the company set the grant date of options granted to new executives in coordination with the release of material nonpublic information?

- Does the company plan to time, or has it timed, its release of material nonpublic information for the purpose of affecting the value of executive compensation?

In addition, discussion of the determination of the stock option exercise price is required if the exercise price is based on the stock's price on a date other than the actual grant date, or the exercise price is determined by using a formula based on average prices (or lowest prices) of the company's stock in a period preceding, surrounding, or following the grant date.

Unlike the compensation committee report, the Compensation Discussion and Analysis is considered soliciting material that is filed with the SEC. As such, this information is subject to the certifications that principal executive officers and principal financial officers are required to make under the Sarbanes-Oxley Act of 2002, as well as the company's disclosure controls and procedures. The Compensation Discussion and Analysis should include the information contained in the tables, footnotes and related narrative, and should cover compensation actions taken in previous years or after the last completed fiscal year end if it enhances the understanding of the disclosure.

Disclosure is not required with respect to specific quantitative or qualitative performance goals involving confidential trade secrets and commercial or financial information that would result in competitive harm to the company. In making this assessment, companies are to apply the same standards used when requesting confidential treatment of trade secrets and commercial or financial information from the SEC, without having to make an actual request. However, if such performance goals are not disclosed, the company must discuss how difficult/likely it will be for the executive/company to achieve the undisclosed goals and the company may be required to demonstrate to the SEC why the disclosure would result in competitive harm. To the extent performance goals have otherwise been publicly disclosed, the nondisclosure exception is not permitted. Disclosure of non-GAAP performance goals is not subject to the general rules regarding disclosure of non-GAAP financial measures, but the company must provide a reconciliation to amounts reported in the audited financial statements.

Summary
Compensation Table

Summary Compensation Table *for the last completed fiscal year ending xx/xx/20xx*

Name and Principal Position	Year	Salary ($)	Bonus ($)	Stock Awards ($)
(a)	(b)	(c)	(d)	(e)

T he rules explicitly require the disclosure of all plan and nonplan compensation awarded to, earned by or paid to the named executive officers, unless specifically excluded by the rules. Examples of compensation that may be excluded from disclosure are nondiscriminatory group life, health, hospitalization and medical reimbursement plans available generally to all salaried employees. Benefits received under relocation plans may not be excluded from disclosure and presumably should be treated as a perquisite, even if non-discriminatory. One or more columns may be omitted if no amounts are reportable for any fiscal year covered by the table.

Year (b)

Information is required for the last three completed fiscal years, or shorter period if not an SEC registrant for all three years. The rules permit a phase-in during the first two years of reporting under the new rules, such that only one year of information is required in the first year and only two years of information are required in the second year.

Salary and Bonus (c) and (d)

Salary and bonus should be based on cash and non-cash amounts that are earned for the applicable fiscal year, regardless of whether paid currently or deferred. These columns should

Option Awards ($)	Nonequity Incentive Plan Compensation ($)	Change in Pension Value & Nonqualified Deferred Compensation Earnings ($)	All Other Compensation ($)	Total ($)
(f)	(g)	(h)	(i)	(j)

include any amount of salary or bonus converted to some other form of non-cash compensation at the election of a named executive officer, with footnote disclosure describing such non-cash compensation and reference to the Grants of Plan-Based Awards table, if applicable. If salary or bonus amounts are not calculable at time of proxy issuance, companies are to provide footnote disclosure stating that fact and the date such amounts are expected to be determined. When the amount is determined, Form 8-K disclosure is required stating the amount and recalculating the total column (j).

Cash bonus awards that are discretionarily or subjectively determined, or not based on pre-established, substantially uncertain and communicated performance criteria are reported in the bonus column (d). Cash bonus awards that are based on pre-established, substantially uncertain and communicated performance criteria must be reported in the nonequity incentive plan compensation column (g), regardless of the duration of the performance period.

Stock and Option Awards (e) and (f)
Column (e) applies to equity and liability awards that do not have option-like features, such as restricted stock and performance shares, and share units. Column (f) applies to

equity and liability awards with option-like features, such as stock options and stock appreciation rights (SARs). For both columns, companies are to disclose the amount of compensation cost recognized for financial statement reporting purposes for the fiscal year in accordance with FAS 123R. This amount includes all or a portion of compensation cost expensed or capitalized in the financial statements for equity and liability awards granted during the last completed fiscal year, as well as for awards granted in previous fiscal years, depending on the vesting conditions of the awards. Companies are to disregard any accounting estimates of forfeitures related to service-based vesting conditions, and instead reverse previously reported compensation cost during the fiscal year in which an actual forfeiture occurs (which could result in a negative balance for the applicable column). Companies are to report compensation cost for awards with a performance-based vesting condition based on the probable outcome of achieving the performance condition, with adjustments in later fiscal years to the extent actual experience differs from previous estimates (which could again result in a negative balance to the applicable column). Companies are to include a footnote describing all forfeitures occurring during the fiscal year, as well as assumptions made in the FAS 123R valuation by making reference to the financial statements, footnotes to the financial statements, or Management's Discussion and Analysis.

Nonequity Incentive Plan Compensation (g)

Represents cash amounts earned in connection with short-term and long-term nonequity incentive plan awards that do not fall within the scope of FAS 123R, such as performance-based annual bonus and performance unit awards. In general, nonequity incentive plan awards are reported in this column only if they are in no way linked to the underlying value of the company's stock. That is, the awards are not denominated in company stock, the award vesting conditions are not based on the company's stock price or the award payment or settlement provisions are not made in company stock. All earnings on nonequity incentive plan compensation (including amounts attributable to any outstanding awards) must be identified and quantified in a footnote and are reportable even if not payable until a later year.

Change in Pension Value & Nonqualified Deferred Compensation Earnings (h)

Represents the sum of (1) the aggregate year-over-year increase in the actuarial present value of accumulated pension benefits under all tax-qualified and supplemental nonqualified defined benefit plans (but excluding tax-qualified and nonqualified defined contribution plans), and (2) above-market or preferential earnings on nonqualified deferred compensation and defined contribution plans. Such amounts should be separately identified and quantified in footnotes and any negative change in pension value should be disclosed in footnotes but not reported in column (h).

Increase in pension value is calculated as the difference between the amount reported in column (d) of the Pension Benefits table for the last completed fiscal year and the amount reported in the same column/table for the next preceding fiscal year, and includes increases in value due to additional years of service, compensation increases and plan amendments (if any), and increases (or decreases) in value attributable to interest.

Interest is above-market if in excess of 120 percent of the applicable federal long-term rate at the date the rate is set or discretionarily reset, with compounding that corresponds most closely to that of the plan. Only the above-market portion of interest is reported, assuming satisfaction of all conditions necessary to receive the highest plan rate. Dividends and dividend equivalents on stock-denominated deferred compensation are preferential if in excess of amounts paid on common stock. Only the preferential portion of dividends and dividend equivalents is reported.

All Other Compensation (i)

Represents amounts not properly reportable in any other column, including the incremental cost to the company of perquisites (unless less than $10,000), tax gross-ups (regardless of amount), company contributions to qualified and nonqualified defined contribution plans, preferential stock purchase discounts (other than discount stock purchase plans available to all salaried employees or dividend reinvestment plans available to all shareholders), preferential insurance premiums, dividends or other earnings not factored into the grant date fair value of stock or option awards and amounts paid or accrued in connection with termination of employment or change-in-control (including defined benefit payments that are accelerated upon change in control).

For the most recently completed fiscal year, all perquisites must be identified if the aggregate amount is $10,000 or more, and each perquisite in excess of $25,000 (or 10 percent of all perquisites, if greater) must be quantified, with footnote disclosure of the company's incremental cost valuation methodology. In addition, for the most recently completed fiscal year, all items other than perquisites in this column must be identified and quantified if in excess of $10,000. Tabular presentation of this column is encouraged under plain English principles if doing so enhances disclosure.

Total (j)

All amounts in this table must be reported as a single numerical value in U.S. dollars, with footnote disclosure of any necessary exchange rate conversions. This table must include all amounts earned, including director fees, regardless of whether paid currently or deferred.

Narrative Disclosure

Narrative disclosure is required of the material factors necessary to gain an understanding of the amounts disclosed in the Summary Compensation Table, including material terms of employment agreements, method of calculating earnings on deferred compensation, and an explanation of salary and bonus in proportion to total compensation.

All Other Compensation

All Other Compensation *(not required; example of plain English tabular presentation)*

Name	Perquisites ($)	Tax Grossups ($)	Defined Contribution Savings Plan Company Contributions ($)	Preferential Stock Purchase Discounts ($)
(a)	(b)	(c)	(d)	(e)

Perquisites (b)

An item is not a perquisite if it is integrally and directly related to the performance of the executive's or director's duties. That is, the executive or director needs the personal benefit to do the job. Examples of items not considered perquisites include Blackberry or laptop computer use if the company believes it is an integral part of the executive's or director's duties to be accessible by e-mail.

Conversely, an item is a perquisite if it confers a direct or indirect benefit that has a personal aspect, unless it is generally available on a nondiscriminatory basis to all employees. The fact that an expense may be an ordinary and necessary business expense for tax or other purposes, or that the expense is for the convenience of the company is not relevant. Examples of perquisites include club memberships not used exclusively for business entertainment purposes, personal financial or tax advice, personal travel or use of other property financed by the company, housing or other living expenses, relocation plans

Preferential Insurance Premiums ($)	Dividends Not Factored in Grant Date Fair Value of Equity Awards ($)	Payments in Regard to Termination of Employment ($)	Total ($)
(f)	(g)	(h)	(i)

(even if nondiscriminatory), security provided at personal residence or during personal travel, commuting expenses and discriminatory discounts on company products or services.

Grants of
Plan-Based Awards

Grants of Plan-Based Awards *for the last completed fiscal year ending xx/xx/20xx*

Name	Grant Date	Approval or Action Date, if Different	Nonequity Incentive Plan Awards: Number of Units or Other Rights (#)	Estimated Future Payouts Under Nonequity Incentive Plan Awards		
				Threshold ($)	Threshold ($)	Maximum ($)
(a)	(b)	(if applicable)	(if applicable)	(c)	(d)	(e)

I n general, disclosure for each award reported in this table must be provided in a separate row. If awards are made under more than one plan, the plan under which the award is granted must be identified. This table or one or more columns may be omitted if no amounts are reportable for the last completed fiscal year covered by the table.

Grant Date (b)

If the grant date is different than the date action was taken by the compensation committee or other administering committee, or the board of directors, a separate adjoining column showing that other date must be added between columns (b) and (c).

Estimated Future Payouts Under Nonequity Incentive Plan Awards (c) to (e)

Represents estimated potential future cash payments of short-term and long-term non-equity incentive plan awards that do not fall within the scope of FAS 123R, such as performance-based annual bonus and performance unit awards. If nonequity incentive plan awards are denominated in units or other rights, a separate adjoining column must be added between columns (b) and (c) to quantify the number of units or other rights awarded.

Estimated Future Payouts Under Equity Incentive Plan Awards			All Other Stock Awards: Number of Shares of Stock or Units	All Other Option Awards: Number of Securities Underlying Options	Exercise or Base Price of Option Awards	Closing Price on Date of Grant for Option Awards, if Different	Grant Date Fair Value of Stock and Option Awards
Threshold (#)	Target (#)	Maximum (#)	(#)	(#)	($)	($)	($)
(f)	(g)	(h)	(i)	(j)	(k)	(if applicable)	(l)

Estimated Future Payouts Under Equity Incentive Plan Awards (f) to (h)

Represents estimated potential future number of share/share unit payments of short-term and long-term equity incentive plan awards that fall within the scope of FAS 123R, such as performance- or market-based stock options and performance shares. Disclosure is also required for repriced or materially modified option awards, except for repricings that occur in connection with a pre-existing formula, an antidilution provision or a recapitalization transaction.

Estimated Future Target Payouts Under Nonequity and Equity Incentive Plan Awards (d) and (g)

If an incentive plan award provides only for a single estimated payout, companies are to report that amount in target columns (d) or (g), as appropriate. If an incentive plan award target is not determinable, companies are to report a representative amount based on the previous fiscal year's performance in columns (d) or (g), as appropriate.

All Other Stock and Option Awards (i) and (j)

Represents the number of stock and option awards granted that are not subject to a performance or market condition, such as service-based restricted stock and stock options (that is, nonincentive plan equity awards). Disclosure is also required for repriced or materially modified option awards, except for repricings that occur in connection with a pre-existing formula, an antidilution provision or a recapitalization transaction. If a nonincentive plan equity award is granted in tandem with an incentive plan award, companies are to report only the nonincentive plan equity award in columns (i) or (j) with accompanying footnote disclosure or textual narrative of the tandem feature, as appropriate.

Exercise or Base Price of Option Awards (k)

If the exercise price is less than the closing price of the company's stock on the grant date, a separate adjoining column must be added between columns (k) and (l) showing the closing price and accompanying footnote disclosure or textual narrative is required to explain the methodology for determining the exercise or base price if different than the closing price. Footnote disclosure is also required if any consideration is paid by the named executive officer for the award.

Grant Date Fair Value of Stock and Option Awards (l)

Represents the grant date fair value of each equity award granted during the last completed fiscal year computed in accordance with FAS 123R, including the incremental fair value of repriced or materially modified option awards (except for repricings that occur in connection with a pre-existing formula, an antidilution provision or a recapitalization transaction).

Narrative Disclosure

Narrative disclosure is required of the material factors necessary to gain an understanding of the amounts disclosed in the Grants of Plan-Based Awards table, including equity award repricings or other material modifications during the last completed fiscal year (such as extensions to the exercise period or changes to the vesting schedule), vesting and earnout schedules and dividend treatment.

Outstanding Equity Awards at Fiscal Year End

Outstanding Equity Awards at Fiscal Year End
for the last completed fiscal year ending xx/xx/20xx

	Option Awards			
Name	Number of Securities Underlying Unexercised Options: Exercisable (#)	Number of Securities Underlying Unexercised Options: Unexercisable (#)	Equity Incentive Plan Awards: Number of Securities Underlying Unexercised Unearned Options (#)	Option Exercise Price ($)
(a)	(b)	(c)	(d)	(e)

In general, outstanding unearned stock and option awards with time-vesting conditions (that is, nonincentive plan equity awards) are reportable in columns (b), (c), (g) and (h), as appropriate. Included in these columns are unexercised option awards and nonvested stock awards previously reported as equity incentive plan awards but that have been subsequently earned. Outstanding unearned stock and option awards with performance-vesting conditions (that is, equity incentive plan awards) are reportable in columns (d), (i), and (j), as appropriate. This table or one or more columns may be omitted if no amounts are reportable for the last completed fiscal year covered by the table.

Options Awards (b) to (f)

Outstanding option awards must be reported on an award-by-award basis (including separate tranches of a single award), unless the exercise price and expiration date are identical (in which case, the awards may be aggregated). This disclosure

		Stock Awards		
Option Expiration Date	Number of Shares or Units of Stock that Have Not Vested (#)	Market Value of Shares or Units of Stock that Have Not Vested ($)	Equity Incentive Plan Awards: Number of Unearned Shares, Units or Other Rights that Have Not Vested (#)	Equity Incentive Plan Awards: Market or Payout Value of Unearned Shares, Units or Other Rights that Have Not Vested ($)
(f)	(g)	(h)	(i)	(j)

should include option awards that have been transferred without value, such as by gifts or other transfers where the executive receives no consideration for the award.

Stock Awards (g) to (j)
Outstanding stock awards are aggregated and reported as a single row, with aggregate market value based on the closing market stock price at the end of the last completed fiscal year.

Vesting Dates and Transferability (b) to (j)
Footnote disclosure is required to identify the vesting dates for each outstanding award, and to identify any awards that have been transferred without value.

Equity Incentive Plan Awards (d), (i), and (j)
Equity incentive plan awards reported in columns (d), (i), or (j) are based on achievement of threshold performance, except that if the previous fiscal year's performance exceeds threshold, the next higher level of performance (that is, either

target or maximum) should be reported. If an award provides only for a single estimated payout, companies are to report that amount. If an award target is not determinable, companies are to report a representative amount based on the previous fiscal year's performance.

Option Exercises
and Stock Vested

Option Exercises and Stock Vested

for the last completed fiscal year ending xx/xx/20xx

	Option Awards		Stock Awards	
Name	Number of Shares Acquired on Exercise (#)	Value Realized on Exercise ($)	Number of Shares Acquired on Vesting (#)	Value Realized on Vesting ($)
(a)	(b)	(c)	(d)	(e)

In general, disclosure must be provided on an aggregate basis for each named executive officer, and includes both nonincentive (for example, time-vesting stock options and restricted stock) and incentive (for example, performance-vesting stock options and performance shares) plan equity awards. This table or one or more columns may be omitted if no amounts are reportable for the last completed fiscal year covered by the table.

Value Realized on Exercise and Vesting (c) and (e)

Value realized is the difference between the market value of the stock at the exercise/vesting date and the exercise or base price (if any). Value realized includes amounts received in connection with an award transfer for value and excludes other payments or consideration received upon exercise/vesting (such as payment of exercise price or related taxes) that are properly reportable in the all other compensation column (i) of the Summary Compensation Table. Footnote disclosure is required to quantify and describe the terms of any amounts realized that are deferred.

Pension Benefits

Pension Benefits *for the last completed fiscal year ending xx/xx/20xx*

Name	Plan Name	Number of Years Credited Service (#)	Present Value of Accumulated Benefit (#)	Payments During Last Fiscal Year ($)
(a)	(b)	(c)	(d)	(e)

In general, disclosure is required for all tax-qualified and supplemental nonqualified defined benefit plans. This table does not require disclosure with respect to tax-qualified and nonqualified defined contribution plans. Benefit allocation between tax-qualified and supplemental nonqualified plans is based on IRS limitations as of the applicable financial statement measurement date. This table or one or more columns may be omitted if no amounts are reportable for any fiscal year covered by the table.

Plan Name (b)
Disclosure for each plan must be provided in a separate row.

Number of Years Credited Service (c)
Computed as of the same measurement date used for financial statement purposes for the last completed fiscal year. If the number of years of service credited under a plan differs from the actual years of service worked, companies are to provide footnote disclosure quantifying the difference and any resulting change in benefits.

Present Value of Accumulated Benefit (d)
Computed as of the same measurement date and applying the same assumptions as used for financial statement purposes for the last completed fiscal year, except for retirement age which

is assumed to be normal retirement age as defined in the plan (or if not so defined, the earliest date retirement can occur with no benefit reduction due to age). Accompanying narrative must disclose the valuation methodology and material assumptions, or make reference to the financial statements, footnotes to financial statements or Management's Discussion and Analysis.

Payments (e)

Represents the dollar value of any payments and benefits paid to the named executive officers during the last completed fiscal year.

Narrative Disclosure

Narrative disclosure is required of the material factors necessary to gain an understanding of the plans disclosed in the Pension Benefits table, including the material terms and conditions of payments and benefits available under the plan, early retirement provisions (if any), specific elements of compensation covered by the pension formula (for example, salary, bonus, etc.), the different purposes for each plan, and any policies for granting extra years of credited service.

Nonqualified Deferred Compensation

Nonqualified Deferred Compensation
for the last completed fiscal year ending xx/xx/20xx

Name	Executive Contributions in Last Fiscal Year ($)	Registrant Contributions in Last Fiscal Year ($)	Aggregate Earning in Last Fiscal Year ($)	Aggregate Withdrawals/ Distributions in Last Fiscal Year ($)	Aggregate Balance at Last Fiscal Year End ($)
(a)	(b)	(c)	(d)	(e)	(f)

In general, disclosure is required for all nonqualified deferred compensation and defined contribution plans. This table does not require disclosure with respect to tax-qualified defined contribution plans, or tax-qualified and nonqualified defined benefit plans. This table or one or more columns may be omitted if no amounts are reportable for any fiscal year covered by the table.

Column (d)

Companies must report all earnings on nonqualified deferred compensation, not just above-market or preferential amounts that are required to be reported in column (h) of the Summary Compensation Table. Where plan earnings are calculated by referenced to actual earnings of mutual funds or other securities, such as company stock, it is sufficient to identify the reference security and quantify its return.

Columns (b) to (f)

Footnote disclosure is required quantifying the extent to which amounts reported in columns (b), (c) and (d) are reported as compensation in the Summary Compensation Table for the last completed fiscal year and the extent to which amounts reported in columns (f) were reported as compensation the Summary Compensation Table for previous years.

Narrative Disclosure

Succinct narrative disclosure is required of the material factors necessary to gain an understanding of the plans disclosed in the Nonqualified Deferred Compensation table, including the types of compensation that may be deferred (and any limitations on the extent to which deferral is allowed), measures for calculating interest or other plan earnings (including whether or not measures are selected by the participant or the company and how often the selection may be changed), interest rates or earnings measures used during the previous fiscal year, and the material terms with respect to payments, withdrawals and other distributions.

Potential Payments upon Termination or Change in Control

The rules require companies to identify and quantify all potential compensation payments at, following, or in connection with any termination of employment. These termination scenarios include voluntary resignation, actual or constructive termination without cause, normal or early retirement or change in control. The $100,000 payment threshold that existed under prior disclosure rules is eliminated. The rules require the following information:

- Explain specific circumstances that would trigger payments
- Describe and quantify the estimated payments and benefits upon each triggering event (except that if a triggering event has actually occurred, disclosure is only required for that specific triggering event)
- Describe and explain how various payment triggers determine payment levels
- Describe and explain any restrictive covenants applicable to receipt of payments, including noncompete, nonsolicitation, nondisparagement or confidentiality agreements
- Describe any other material factors.

For purposes of quantifying payments, the triggering event is assumed to take place on the last business day of the last completed fiscal year based on the closing market stock price at that date. Reasonable estimates (or a reasonable estimated range of amounts) are required in event uncertainties exist. Perquisites are to be included in the quantification of payments if $10,000 or more in the aggregate and health-care benefits should be valued using the same assumptions as for financial statement purposes. Disclosure is not required with respect to contracts, agreements or arrangements to the extent they do not discriminate in scope, terms, or operation and are available generally to all salaried employees. Tabular presentation is encouraged under plain English principles if it enhances disclosure.

Director Compensation

Director Compensation *for the last completed fiscal year ending xx/xx/20xx*

Name	Fees Earned or Paid in Cash ($)	Stock Awards ($)	Option Awards ($)
(a)	(b)	(c)	(d)

I f the director is also a named executive officer, report all director compensation amounts in the Summary Compensation Table (and not in this table), with footnote disclosure in that table indicating what amounts are attributable to services as a director. One or more columns may be omitted if no amounts are reportable for the last completed fiscal year covered by the table.

Fees Earned or Paid in Cash (b)
Represents all cash fees earned or paid, including annual retainer fees, committee and/or chairmanship fees and meeting fees.

Stock and Option Awards (c) and (d)
Represents generally the same disclosures required for columns (e) and (f) of the Summary Compensation Table for executives. Companies are to provide footnote disclosure for each director of the grant date fair value of each equity award granted during the last completed fiscal year computed in accordance with FAS 123R (including the incremental fair value of repriced or materially modified option awards), and the aggregate number of stock and option awards outstanding at fiscal year end.

Columns (e) to (g)
Represents generally the same disclosures required for columns (g) to (i) of the Summary Compensation Table for executives.

Nonequity Incentive Plan Compensation ($)	Change in Pension Value & Nonqualified Deferred Compensation Earnings ($)	All Other Compensation ($)	Total ($)
(e)	(f)	(g)	(h)

Companies are to include in column (g) consulting fees paid by the company (including fees paid by subsidiaries and/or joint ventures), and legacy and similar charitable award program benefits.

Total (h)

All amounts in this table must be reported as a single numerical value in U.S. dollars, with footnote disclosure of any necessary exchange rate conversions. This table must include all amounts earned, regardless of whether paid currently or deferred. Two or more directors may be grouped in a single row if all elements of compensation for each director are identical.

Narrative Disclosure

Narrative disclosure is required of the material factors necessary to gain an understanding of the amounts disclosed in the Director Compensation table, including a description of fees for retainer, committee service, service as chairman of the board or a committee, meeting attendance, and any different compensation arrangements for a particular director. Tabular presentation is encouraged under plain English principles if it enhances disclosure.

Other Related Disclosures

Securities Ownership of Management

Companies are required to provide plain English tabular presentation of the number and percentage of shares of each class of company stock beneficially owned by each of the named executive officers and directors and by all executive officers and directors as a group. For purposes of this disclosure, beneficial ownership is defined as shares of company stock over which the executive or director has sole or shared voting power, and/or sole or shared investment/disposition power (as opposed to economic or pecuniary interest). In addition, beneficial ownership also includes company shares that may be acquired within 60 days of the record date through the exercise of stock options or the conversion of stock units into actual stock. Thus, shares considered beneficially owned include shares owned outright, restricted stock, shares covered by vested and payable stock options/SARs or stock units, and shares covered by stock options/SARs or stock units that will vest and become payable within 60 days of the record date. Shares not considered beneficially owned include cash-settled SARs or stock units, and stock-settled stock units that are not payable until more than 60 days after the record date. The rules require additional disclosure of the number of shares that are beneficially owned that have been pledged as security (if any).

Transactions with Related Persons

The rules require principles-based plain English disclosure of any transaction or proposed transaction since the beginning of the last completed fiscal year in excess of $120,000 in which the company is a participant, and in which a related person has a direct or indirect material interest. Related persons are defined generally as executive officers, directors, greater than five percent shareholders or any immediate family members of each of the above persons. In addition, the rules require companies to disclose their policies for review and approval of related person transactions.

Equity Compensation Plan Information

The SEC requires companies to include tabular information about two categories of equity compensation plans in their annual reports, as well as in their proxy statements in years when submitting a compensation plan for shareholder approval. The two categories of equity compensation plans are plans that have been approved by shareholders, and plans that have not. With respect to each category, companies must disclose the number of shares to be issued upon option exercise or share issuance for all outstanding awards under all plans, the weighted average exercise price of outstanding stock options, and the number of shares remaining available for future issuance under all equity compensation plans in effect as of the end of the last completed fiscal year. Companies are further required to identify and briefly describe the material features of each equity compensation plan in effect as of the end of the last completed fiscal year that was not approved by shareholders.

Form 8-K Disclosures

The rules revise the reporting requirements of Form 8-K to generally require companies to provide a brief description of the material terms of compensatory arrangements entered into or materially modified in connection with the following triggering events:

- Departure of certain officers, named executive officers and directors
- Appointment of certain officers and election of directors

- Adoption or material modification of material compensatory arrangements for named executive officers (but not directors)

- Payment of salary or bonus previously omitted from the Summary Compensation Table for named executive officers.

Certain officers are defined as the principal executive officer, president, principal financial officer, principal accounting officer, principal operating officer or any person performing similar functions. Form 8-K filing is required within four business days of the triggering event.

Form 10-Q and 10-K Exhibits

The following executive and director compensation arrangements are required to be filed as exhibits to Forms 10-Q or 10-K:

- Any management contract or any compensatory plan, contract, or arrangement, including but not limited to plans relating to options, warrants or rights, pension, retirement, or deferred compensation or bonus, incentive or profit sharing (or if not set forth in any formal document, a written description thereof) in which any director or any named executive officer participates and any other management contract or any other compensatory plan, contract or arrangement in which any other executive officer of the company participates unless immaterial in amount or significance.

- Any compensatory plan, contract or arrangement adopted without the approval of security holders pursuant to which equity may be awarded, including, but not limited to, options, warrants or rights (or if not set forth in any formal document, a written description thereof), in which any employee (whether or not a executive officer of the company) participates unless immaterial in amount or significance.

Companies must provide an exhibit index identifying all existing plans, arrangements, and contracts, and citing the prior or current SEC filing in which the specific document was submitted as an exhibit.

Shareholder Approval of New or Amended Plans

Finally, there is additional proxy statement disclosure when a company is soliciting shareholder approval to adopt new compensation or benefits plans or to make amendments to existing plans. A summary of the plans or amendments must be provided. If the amounts of future benefits or deliverable awards can be determined, then they also must be disclosed in tabular format.